Snow Angels on the Living Room Floor

poems by

Sara Ries

Finishing Line Press
Georgetown, Kentucky

Snow Angels on the Living Room Floor

For Thaddeus
with whom I don't have skin

ACKNOWLEDGMENTS

Poems in this collection have appeared in the following publications,
sometimes in earlier versions and I gratefully acknowledge these editors.

"Snow Angels on the Living Room Floor" in *Iconoclast*
"dead of winter" and "Grandma's Railing" in *Earth's Daughters*
"Mango Phone Conversation" in *Come In, We're Open*
"Namaste" and "Mr. Bojangles" in *The Buffalo News*
"Conesus Lake, Midnight" in *Blast Furnace*
"Old Man Spider" in *Nomad*
"The Day I Learned to Let in Noise" and "3:34 A.M." in *Brigid's Fire, The
    South Buffalo Anthology of Poetry*
"Old Man Spider" and "Namaste" in *Steelbellow*
"Christmas is Three Days Away and It's Raining" and "Becoming Waves" in
    A Celebration of Western New York Poets
"Artist Café, Cachoeira" forthcoming in *Secret Destinations: Chatham
University MFA Field Seminar Writings 2003-2018*

Publisher: Leah Maines
Editor: Christen Kincaid
Cover Art: George Grace
Author Photo: Thaddeus Edward Ries Dziekonski
Cover Design: Leah Huete

Printed in the USA on acid-free paper.
Order online: www.finishinglinepress.com
        also available on amazon.com

Author inquiries and mail orders:
Finishing Line Press
P. O. Box 1626
Georgetown, Kentucky 40324
U. S. A.

Table of Contents

Snow Angels on the Living Room Floor

The night before I left for grad school
you gave me a napkin poem that read
I love you. A friend said *Careful,*
he's telling you this now?
but I knew it was just our story.

My poetry mentor said, raising my poems
in her hand, *It's working out well for your poetry.*
You have a theme here: longing.

It was then that I fell in love with the word *longing,*
the way my tongue touches the back of my front teeth
to sound the *l,* how the *o* opens my mouth,
lets the hot breath out.

Late night phone conversation,
a month into Pittsburgh, I said:

So I had this dream, Thaddeus. We were in my living room
and our hands were freezing, but it was summer.
You said 'Come here, to the free heat'
so we stood by the radiator,
you behind me, your hands covering mine
blowing breath on our hands.

From your bed in Buffalo,
voice deep and hours away
you knew why our hands were cold.

Because, you said, *in my dream*
you swung open the freezer door and said
'Look, Thaddeus, I saved some snow from winter'
and we made snow angels on your living room floor.

It was then that I believed in longing,
knelt and folded my hands,
giving my life to it.

The Whole Song

I love the lyrics, I say for the fifth time
driving under a sky swollen with moon,
but you never hear the lyrics
and once again you ask, *What are they?*

You were fixed on the saxophone
trailing off onto an unmarked highway.
Miles ago the piano sounds swirled
around stars in the royal blue sky.

Last night we slept like shoes in a box.
I'd like to hear you play trumpet, I say,
and you murmur, *When the time is right.*

You park the car; headlights
make trails across the river
and with one click—they're gone.

This river is close to my heart, you say.
We stand still watching the water
run fiercely to Niagara Falls.
You tell me *Those tiny whirlpools are us.*

Finally, our favorite eddy reaches the falls
and I hear your music
for the first time as I shower.

Ear to the living room, I stand
drenched in your notes, unaware of my words
forming puddles by my feet.

Mr. Bojangles

You were most beautiful
the morning you danced and played your trumpet
to *Mr. Bojangles* in the living room,
your soft white robe a light around you.

I was watering our giant sunflowers on the balcony,
wishing the moment would stretch on
but the phone rang,

and you set your trumpet
down,

and the moment withered or shriveled
severed
from the string of life it sprung from.

   So I stood there with my empty watering can,
an invisible cord tugging me toward the faucet

but I stayed still, planted,
begging that moment back.

Artist Café, Cachoeira

I want to be more outside my skin,
I write in my journal between sips
of caipirinha. I check and recheck my bag
for map, wallet, hotel key, then scrawl
My skin is a door cracked open; I must remember
it's not a border. My pen runs out of ink,

so I order another cocktail. The bartender asks me
something in Portuguese, amused that I don't understand,
that I could be sitting right here on this bar stool
where countless Brazilians have mingled,
but the landscape of my language is different.
He scribbles "gringa" on my guest check.

Everyone sings a song they all know—
I should at least hum along, should at least sway
but I tell myself *No, they might laugh*
at how this gringa grooves.

But my feet disagree, tapping to the beat
of the tan-tan—I don't want even my feet taps seen
so I press my soles to the floor; lifting my feet would be
like driving under a thin moon with no headlights.
For a few strums of the cavaquinho, they stay still,
but after another sip of caipirinha, they start up again
                    tap tap tapping
against the hardwood floor.
The sweaty red-faced crowd raises their drinks
and when they reach their favorite verse, glasses clink
and they're shouting the lyrics through fits of laughter,
wild-eyed disciples of joy.

                    The band motions for me to dance.
                    I say no but my body springs up;

and for some beats, I don't judge
my body's interpretation of rhythm.
I once looked at my body and thought:
separate—but tonight,

the door of my skin has swung open.

Old Man Spider

has a bulging belly
and bent needle legs.
At the grocery store café,
while the jazz band plays,
he finishes his fish fry, and stuffs
greasy napkins into a paper cup.
A hospital bracelet dangles
from the curve of his cane,
and I want someone to tear off
his mismatched toupee,
look him in the eyes, tell him:
we are not as separate
as it seems.

From a mustard-stained shirt pocket,
he pulls out a phone, presses it to
his ear hairs. *It's me,* he says
as his fat finger flicks
crumbs off the table.
Over the trumpet, he shouts
Just had a fish fry. Mac salad's plain
but the fish is fresh—
I picked one up for you.
A man with bushy black eyebrows yells
I'm trying to hear the band!

Can I bring over your fish? Old Man Spider
asks, finger shutting the other ear.
Some change tables; others huff.
What? Oh. I see, he says. *Ok. Ok.*
Bye then and slips his phone back
into his mustard-stained pocket,
grabs his cane to get up,
but his legs won't work
so a boy passing by yanks him up
like a sack of flour,
then brushes his own skin
as if there were spiders.

Mango Phone Conversation

I tell you with my back against polka dot bed sheets
feet traveling up the cold white wall:
All I want to do is eat dried mangoes with you.

Don't like dried fruit, you say
like to cut it in thin even slices.

It's not about mangoes, dammit.
You don't have to eat them.

You reply:
That is like brushing our teeth at the same time
but in different rooms, forever.

The Day I Learned to Let in Noise

Third grade fire drill:
My ugly sneakers are exactly behind Andy's
cool Converse as we shuffle down the hall.
Single file, Ms. Smith hollers, high heels hammering
along the jagged stream of our bodies
until we become an arrow pointed to the door
at the end of the hall.

My fingers protect my ears from that little red box
that screams and shakes my teeth loose.
Teacher's dress swooshes her calves;
heels click at me—*Grow up,* she says,
shaking her head, arms crossed.

Sorry, I say, put down my hands
and they hang, two apples
rotten on my branches.

I want to go back to that girl as the woman I am now,
tell her: *Dear child, block the noise, some sounds
kill*—But I know she'd only mumble
It's okay, then wait for the outdoors, where wind strums grass blades,

a harp in the sunlight, and the alarm
is but a few jingled coins. She will go on, letting in
the world's cold stark notes.

Broken Swing Rondeau

The snow has nearly erased this swing set
here in the park, where somewhere, a wand and barrette
are buried in white. I'm the only human footprint,
brushing off a swing to sit. When my mittens
grip the chains, I remember my secret:

My cousin and I were ten, and for once, I was swinging the highest,
shouting *Look how high*—when my seat cracked. My body slammed
into mud. *Sorry for my big bones*, I sobbed to my aunt in the kitchen
    (the snow has failed to erase this memory)

and she handed me a black bag bigger than me, said
Take out the trash. I give this memory back, and pretend
that now I can reach the treetops, where my feet point.
Body slicing time, I am in the deep end,
as the sky unwinds the last shreds of sunset
      not even snow can erase.

3:34 A.M.

Wind keeps knocking on windows.
You splay the book, step outside. Your body
sways and cracks to a lullaby for insomniacs
composed by crickets.

You can't dance, an ex once shouted
when your high heel spiked his bare toe—
you were about to make love.

You fling off slippers as if they could knock
down memories, dance across back yards,
unsure if the grass is damp or cold.

Dancing:
to move through the door of yourself.

Under a moon made of communion bread
windows are black, snorers breathe songs
of slumber, and you, in midnight silk pajamas
are the wind's dance partner
sailing across the ocean
of grass.

South

Winding through
the mountains,
I worry that your hands,
firm on the steering wheel,
know something
more than mine
or maybe they just take driving
or life
more seriously.
Your knuckles are calloused
from leaning on the cutting board,
waiting for souvlaki
and steaks to cook.
Our whole lives,
we wait for something.

My feet sticky
on the windshield,
I form words
in my little black journal.
I tell you
The words are not the feeling
and you say *Yeah?*
then change the station.
We drive south for a wedding.
I write: *treetop bits dappled across sky,*
pieces of sky for leaves,
hands with everybody's in them—
Alone would not be a word, then.
I stare at my leg tattoos; your touch
brings me back to us.

I wipe my forehead sweat
on your thigh;
you squeeze my knee.
Once, when I was younger,
after complaining about
summer heat, my dad said
You think this is hot,
imagine what hell must feel like—

even then I knew that fear
slams the doors on ourselves,
in these dances of grit
and longing.

Becoming Waves

We drove for hours
up the California coast
as the ocean stretched by.

Sherri lit a cigarette,
turned up another song
I didn't know.

I kept my eyes shut, sick to see
so much borderless blue
and not go in.

When Sherri finally parked,
I ran to the ocean in my bright red bathing suit.
Just me, the sand, and all those shades of blue.
As I reached the shore, Sherri snapped this picture.

Look at me, a blood stain on a blue blouse,
arms outstretched, about to be swallowed,
wanting more than anything to be swallowed.

If you look long enough,
the waves will turn me into them,
love me that much.

Oranges

For days, Mom calls, says
Could you use oranges?

Two cases in two weeks were sent
from the uncle who eats Spam and noodles
every night for dinner, and who once told me

he broke up with a woman when she proposed to him,
because men should ask women,
and that love is best seen through Catholicism.

He sends them often, even though
we're an apple family.
I've never even seen my parents peel an orange.

Only certain hands
can successfully peel an orange.
The too old and too young, the arthritic,
and the ones with frail fingernails, are left out.

My fridge is too small for condiments
and peeling them bends my fingernails
but I say *I'll take some,* then store bagfuls
in my cobwebbed closet.

Morning. Sunless.
I'm afraid my words are oranges, when I need
words like water, to pour off the page
and quench people.

I chuck my pen against
the wall, but the ink won't explode.
I storm to the kitchen and slice
all the oranges—I squeeze the guts from them:
six glasses, which I drink at once,
no stubborn skin between us.

My mother calls me, tired of oranges.
Tired of oranges, I mumble *Hello.*
She says *Sara, this time your uncle sent*

tangerines, but only a dozen—
and I knew that my uncle
had become easier
to peel.

Namaste

In India, to greet, we'd fold our hands
against our hearts and say, Namaste. *Namaste*

along forts, mansions, and sand dunes,
beggars all around us,

chai and incense and dal,
babies with empty bottles.

Namaste, we'd say, and fill spaces between us
second syllables rising, then the falling to reach

another body's shore. At home,
I say *hi*; it feels like a surge

from a firefighter's hose
washing the person away.

So I miss the pressing of palms
slight bow of heads

as if nothing else exists.

Still or Rippled

He took another sip of tea, leaned forward, and said *Should the water of life be rippled, or should it be still?* We sat at a smudged glass table, knowing everything in a field of questions, until we gave up on words, letting silence weave uncertainties between us. There were paintbrushes next to canvases and tubes of oil paint. *Paint* he said, but the portrait I formed was blue and weeping, so I brushed it with orange and it became a mud puddle.

Oil paints take five days to dry. You are supposed to give the layers time before they're painted over, but I never do, so I wind up with muddy puddles. Is that how the soul looks when we're impatient, always stuck on yesterday's moment or the moment we can't wait for?

I say, let the water be still and rippled; either way is perfect. And those uncertainties: they are just hitchhikers. Too often I let them in and before I ask *which way,* they've hijacked my body and grabbed the wheel.

Silent Hallelujah
for Lola Haskins

Outside, snow covers grit
the way skin holds sadness in people.

I dash in Vietnamese cinnamon, sprinkle some salt,
pour the sugar, and, when track five begins *Hallelujah*,
I remember

that brutal drive from St. Augustine to Gainesville
sunset burning our eyes. We yanked our visors down,
two shields against an army of light,

Alma's eye already screaming from sunblock
that snuck in. Back at the beach, when I spotted the smear
high on her cheekbone, I should've said something.
We'd sat on towels in hooded sweatshirts blowing breath on our hands
but I had to go—it was January and I'm from Buffalo.

I stared out my window as Alma gripped the wheel,
stinging tears speeding down her cheek.
Every few miles, words shook the silence.

I stared out the window even though Alma was beside me
and for years before we had only handwritten letters
sealed & stamped with longing.

Halfway to Gainesville Alma said,
How about some Leonard? And for a moment,
the sun seemed less severe. Words rippled the silence
like skipping stones into some pond
no one ever bothered to name.

Hallelujah is my favorite song, we exclaimed,
and she turned to me, said *You have to hear
this live version. I sing it at the top of my lungs and sob.*

I felt like a child with a bouquet of balloons.
We listened to the beginning chords of each song until we were back
to the first. *It's on here,* she promised, and the child let go of the strings,
stared at the sky, balloons shrinking to specks.

I love the lyrics, I said, sure we'd find *Hallelujah*
and sing the way we did the night before when we danced
under a crystal chandelier in her living room, lips stained Merlot, laughing.
Her wrinkles were currents of wisdom that flowed from the river
of her body. I squeezed her slender hand, but nothing,
not even my clumsy grip, could stop her from being liquid.
When she spun me beside a shelf, I saw
her name on the row of book spines. I said *Alma*—
then my foot landed on hers. *She said
Shh. It took me years and years and years.*

Cruise control on,
we went through all the songs
again and again, slower each time,
until Alma said *Forget it,* and I said
Maybe another time,
my balloons all disappeared.

I stared at the clouds and imagined
they were trampolines, and I was up there
picking which shapes to spring from.
We turned right, and the sun got left behind.

After too many miles of silence,
Alma said, *Do you know about fire ants?*
No, I said, thinking *Here's another subject
I haven't a clue about,* and she told me something
that made me say *Really? Really?*

but I can't recall a bit of that now
as I slide these cookies into the oven,
wait for them to crisp.

Outside, snow covers swing sets
the way skin holds music in people.

Somebody, write me a song
for all the songs that were lost
when we needed them, and for the songs
that delivered themselves to us

but we weren't ready,
stuck on skipping notes
from yesterday.

The Story That Will Save Us

I need words, I thought.
You sat there with calm eyes
and closed lips.
What must be the door of you.

I'm tired of filling our spaces with chatter.
You moved your lips (only to smile)
and I began to create your dialogue.

Until I decided to let silence speak,
(which I read somewhere,)
and the moments became a book
I analyzed for a plot,
but something said *Stop*.

And because I sat long enough to fill
our space with silence,
I saw that nothing really happened,
and that's the story that will save us.

Conesus Lake, Midnight

We walk
the white dock
slowly,
as if the end
were an altar
and the waves
in their black robes
would rise up
to pronounce us
man and wife.

We hold hands,
our eyes pointed to the script of sky:
The Hunter shines his sword;
The Great Bear lumbers toward the moon,
a circle. Our feet go on, even though
one wrong step and the old lake,
with all its stories, would drink us.

At the altar, we sit
and shed our shoes
dip our toes into
cold navy blue
and our feet,
from the current,
become lopsided
pendulums.

I connect the lights from the sky
and the houses across the lake in cursive.
I make them say: *Yes, I see you*
holding hands, brushing feet.

We are still touching
our bare blind feet,
two substantial specks
under an endless sky,

and the dark is not so deep
and filled with hunger.

dead of winter

hands held, we trudge through the kind of cold
that reminds us just how small we are.
our free palms grip hand warmers;
the rest of us stiffens with each creak of snow.
our goal, i say, is for our joined hands
to become warmer than our packet-heated hands.
pretend we're colors, bodiless.
i'm magenta; you're forest green, and all we do is blend
though sometimes skin gets in the way.
i step my numb feet hard on littered snow
and wait for words, for thin flames to flicker from your lips.
you lower your head and sigh.
on the eleventh step, you
press your mouth to the cluster of our clenched fingers.

Grandma's Railing

I.

As a child, I sat on Grandma's bed
and watched her dancer fingers
twirl her grays round a pen,
then dip in a worn bag for a bobby pin.
But now, at my garbage-picked dinner table,
we're all thrown off by Grandma's hair,
an old rag on a hook. I swallow wrong, cough
and say *Grams, how come your hair's straight?*
Her fork slips from her hand, falls to her lap
on a stretcher made of napkin.
Her eyes brake at my pony tail.
She says *Curling hair takes energy*
and I picture a girl shoving her hips
into a too-tight dress.

II.

It took twenty-two songs for Grandma
to climb my three flights of stairs
but Grams wanted to see my home.
Her cane poked like a lost dog.
She refused my hand. Twice.
I said *We could go to a restaurant,*
and she said *That won't be necessary.*
Her spindly fingers pressed
the wall for something. Dad said
This would all be easier if you had a railing,
then extended his calloused hand and said
Mother, please, take my hand. She said *I don't need
your hand,* and stayed with the wall
like the last lover she will ever touch.

Grandma's foot shook midair
until Dad extended his arm and said
Let me be your railing. It took a few seconds
for the new picture to shift and fit in Grandma's mind.
Then she put her hand on Dad's arm, said

As though it was a railing, laughed and said again and again
As though   it was a railing.   As though it was   a railing
all the way to the top.

Prayer for an Insomniac

In the morning, when the sun tips its hat
then tap dances the Shirley Temple
across your wooden floor,

having squeezed through the gaps
of curtains and window panes
that you franticly blocked
with blankets and duct tape

and a thin tank top
shaped like a snake
and shielding your eyes,

you bow to your feather pillow,
holder of snot and tears.

Don't change the sheets,
your record of tosses and turns
and crashed carpet rides.

Not even your lover can bestow
whatever magic mixes in the brain
to sail one off to sleep.

You'll never be ready, so get up.
Sleep is not your destination.

Smooth and fold the sleep shirt,
gently place the earplugs back
into their perfect cylindrical case.
Kiss the hood of the sweatshirt
that tried to dim your mind's light.

Then, yank the curtain open and face
that stinging yellow river which pulls
freighters and little plastic boats
alike.

Stinky Sweater Sestina

The poet finally loves her gums that have receded
the hairs tangled in toothpaste
stink bug falling from a holiday sweater,
first time off the hanger since last year.
She believes snow on trees equals magic
so she stays in pajamas, pretends it's a snow day.

Bad Penny is out dancing again today
in every dive in town. She recedes
from shots too late, fast dancing with magic.
She chases whiskey with wasabi paste,
shimmies and declares, *I'll dance until my dying year*
then flings her sparkly cigarette-stained sweater.

Girlfriend, not the yellow sweater!
he yells from the kitchen. *Today*
wear something new. It has softened the cold for years,
so she shouts in its glorious glow, *Too late,* recedes
to the bathroom, unscrews the bubble gum toothpaste.
When he sees Old Yeller again, she mouths, *It's magic.*

Lately all you think about is magic.
You believe magic can be as simple as a sweater
that's loved, ripped and encrusted with toothpaste.
There's more, and it keeps you up for days.
You worry your magic is receding,
swirling away with the years.

Jade's been homeless for over a year.
Have you seen her? Nearly a ghost, life depleted of magic.
She wanders the streets all night; it's safer than receding
to boxes or bridges. She prays to her olive green sweater
and split-soled shoes to survive another day
in this life full of scissors—hurry, deliver paste.

After a breakup he climbs to the summit, pastes
photos to the grass, one from each year
spent together. He picks up the first one, remembers the day
the blossoms began, that kiss, when he first tasted magic,
those high school sweethearts in matching striped sweaters.
He buries it, believing the memory will recede.

We go on, pasting our longings to magic
in our young and years-old sweaters.
One day, let's cradle our fears; maybe then they will recede.

Independent Living Class, Eleventh Grade

Ms. Redder with a blonde bob and rosy cheeks warned
our 'gum smacking, note-passing, too cool for school' class,
Living with somebody can be difficult.
Suppose you like the toilet paper to hang
the way that your roommate can't stand.

I've waited for this conversation.
Thirteen apartments, eighteen roommates, the closest was,
Your turn to buy it. I'd ask myself which way I prefer to hang it,
Like this, and my hand brushes the wall
but that way doesn't look as neat.

Then, after seven years of sharing bath towels,
grilled cheeses and water glasses layered with lip impressions,
Thaddeus holds up the roll and says
So the toilet paper: You put it on the holder this way
but it should really go like this so the paper's easier to tear.

Here, in this apartment on another continent,
wooden beams across cathedral ceilings,
dogs howling in our backyard lumberyard
I see the eleventh grade Me,
wide-legged jeans, chipped nail polish,
hair frizzy from cheap perms:

She is sitting on that hard chair, two legs mid-air,
wondering, hoping, that someday
this topic would come up.

Selling My Childhood Home

I yank open the cardboard flaps of yet another box
lugged up from the basement, pour a glass of Clean Slate Riesling,
chosen by Thaddeus, because all month I've gone through boxes
that have rotted for decades in the musty basement of a childhood home
that's hardly my family's anymore—I saw the realtor stab
the lawn with a Sold sign.

We asked the realtor for a picture of him by the sign.
He said: *My picture's on the sign,*
so that's what we're left with.

Thaddeus gasps at the pile of boxes, says
Growing up, I was given one drawer of a hallway dresser
and anything that didn't fit, I got rid of.

Got rid of.
The phrase alone makes my family uneasy.
We come from a long line of hoarders, but we're
doing well compared to my aunt who has boxes stacked
to ceilings, and paths snaking through them.
My other aunt has filled the spare bathroom
with her late ex-husband's things.

What is it we're afraid to let go of?
Each trinket given away is a page of history.
Lost. We write the story of our lives with objects.
But when rooms become stuffed with pages busting the binding,
we toss them into totes and drag them to the basement.
No one opens the covers—
besides they stink too much.

My mother, watching me throw most things into a trash bag,
attempting to bite her tongue, says, *But Sara—don't you want*
your softball trophies (I played outfield), *and what about your drawing*
of the diner, and you're not giving away that stuffed smiley face
with the graduation cap that everyone signed at your party, are you?
I got that for you.
My dad panics,
Our guest room in Florida is filled with totes!

I tell them about the documentary
called Minimalism.

My childhood dolls look like they belong in coffins.
The Barbies are moldy and missing heads.
Stale school work is crumpled with red ink like bloodied wings.

Thaddeus refills my glass of Clean Slate Riesling.
I open another box of mildewy clothes, and—
a small knit blanket.

That's your baby blanket, my mother tells me
as I unfold it, amazed that it survived.
It's two shades of blue,
morning sky beside midnight.

My mother, wide-eyed at the edge of the couch,
acts like tossing it would be rejecting where I came from.
I know she's replaying a memory of me
in my crib with this blanket.

I set it into a box marked Save, then take it out,
wrap it around my shoulders—
the first thing that held me
when I had to be left alone.

Potato Salad at Midnight

Between living in Colombia and Costa Rica,
you're at your childhood home your parents are scrambling to sell,
trying to erase the clutter of over three decades. Your mother,
on top of the world these days, is up stretching her legs
with a huge grin as you're scooping yourself some potato salad
in the still-quiet night. You're tasting it and telling your mother it's better
than your dad's. Your father comes into the kitchen like the journey of an
    eye drop
from the bottle   into the eye. He's here to retrieve your mother,
who really does need sleep even though she hardly believes it.
Your father is serious, so serious.   *Good potato salad,* you say,
and think: this is a play and we're all actors. Let's shake off this heavy air,
erupt into raucous laughter. Usually you stay in the kitchen to form an
    alliance
with your bright-eyed mother, but this time, you disappear into your room
where your husband is sleeping.
You kiss his marvelous forehead,
      and the stiffness of air falls softly
            like the season's
              first
      snowfall.

First Anniversary Poem

We were a paragraph dressed in white
under mountainous clouds; all day our love climbed

without us. The winds roared their praises,
my veil shot up in agreement.

The trustworthy arms of the Andes squeezed us
like never before. You poured out your trumpet song,

your face so red it shone pieces of your heart.
My wing tattoos fluttered as I walked

the rose-petaled path to meet you,
to recite to you the greatest poem of my life.

All day we sailed in whites,
you in stark white and crimson, me in ivory and silver.

A sunny sprinkle blessed our glistening skin.
We were a capital S and T pulling each other closer.

We loved and we love without punctuation.
We could never be double-spaced for too long,

even at our worst, even when we're blind creatures
crawling on the floor, we find our way back to each other,

and stroll together again
to a rhythm pulsing with our heartbeats.

Christmas Is Three Days Away and It's Raining

You are stage-curtain-tall, hunched at your desk,
flipping through photos to gift. *Next year,* I say,
I think I'll write poems, place them in boxes and wrap them.
You like that idea, so I sculpt these words for you:

Yesterday I burnt the grilled cheeses.
You smiled and said *That's the oldest trick in the book,*
burn dinner so you don't have to make it again.
You were quiet, and I was hungry for words fierce and fresh.

We're in Buffalo, picturing ourselves in South America,
but this is our life right now:
Your trumpet is by the door for band practice
and you, musical you, are whistling as you stir the pasta.
A semester of teaching just ended,
so our table is a scatter of graded essays.
Your dirty socks are boats on the kitchen floor.

Remember you said *I feel like we're mostly in your country*
but you don't always come to mine—I'd like to be in your country more
but my words are waterfalls and yours are hors d'oeuvres.

I store your words like fine china in the cabinets of my mind.
These are years old: *When I see you, all my worries melt away*
like ice cream on a metal mountain.

Christmas is three days away.
I return, drop my bags and umbrella on the couch.
You are hanging a glittery trumpet on the tree.
The whole time shopping, your favorite song was stuck in my head
and now it's playing.

I bought this for my mother, I say,
and hold up a scarf. I decided on the green one even though
I couldn't stop staring at the purple scarf.
My mother would like the green scarf.
You point under the tree, the one we gave a second life to
after it was discarded by the real estate party, and say *Open it.*

It's the same purple scarf from earlier
and you bought it not knowing my want for it.
That's how it is with you.
Even wordless in different countries, we meet.

Sometimes,
before I say goodbye
I dish you some ice cream.

And sometimes,
before you have to leave
you light me a candle.

Additional Acknowledgments

My unending gratitude goes out to my family and friends (too many of you to name) who have offered such blooming kindness and support along the way. Thaddeus, for your unwavering bright light and inspiration; Melissa Lussier, for listening to my poems during our late night phone conversations; and George Grace, who read and commented on a recent version of this manuscript with such care. I am forever thankful for all the beautiful souls of the Buffalo literary community.

A gigantic thanks goes out to those who have edited these poems over the years, sometimes multiple versions: former and present members of the Bad Pudding writing group, including: George and Donna Grace, Kate Willoughby (who also inspired the title), Michael Delaney, Gary Earl Ross, Gene Grabiner, Lynn Ciesielski, Josh Smith, and Patrick Cornelius. Much gratitude to Theresa Wyatt for her close examinations of several of these poems; Ann Goldsmith, for her Saturday morning workshops; Erika Hendra; Lisa Wiley; and Lola Haskins and Angela Kaiser, for their generous blurbs and tremendous support. A special acknowledgement goes out to the wise and warm women of Monday morning's writing group for encouraging me to develop the poem-pieces that I'd write during our journal time. It is because of you that some of these poems got typed and shared in the first place.

Sara Ries is a Buffalo native and holds a BA from the State University of New York at Fredonia and an MFA from Chatham University, where she received the Best Thesis in Poetry Award. This collection of poems about growing up in her parents' diner became her first book, *Come In, We're Open,* which won the Stevens Poetry Manuscript Competition and was published in June 2010 by the NFSPS Press. Her poem, "Fish Fry Daughter," was selected by Ted Kooser for his *American Life in Poetry* column. She taught composition and literature at Erie Community College before moving to South America to teach ESL for SENA, Colombia's public university. She was the co-founder and host of the Poetry & Dinner Night reading series at the Woodlawn Diner, which her parents owned for 32 years. Her poems have appeared in *The Buffalo News, Earth's Daughters, Nomad, Steel Bellow, Blue Collar Review, LABOR: Studies in Working-Class History of the Americas, Words Without Walls: Writers on Addiction, Violence, and Incarceration,* and *A Celebration of Western New York Poets,* among others. She is currently working on a second collection of diner poems and a book about her time spent in the lovely land of Colombia.